# Series TV

Cast and crew crowd behind the camera as they watch a scene being filmed.

# Series TV

## How a Television Show Is Made

by Malka Drucker and
Elizabeth James

## Clarion Books
TICKNOR & FIELDS: A HOUGHTON MIFFLIN COMPANY
New York

Clarion Books
Ticknor & Fields, a Houghton Mifflin Company
Copyright © 1983 by Malka Drucker and Elizabeth James

*Library of Congress Cataloging in Publication Data*
Drucker, Malka.
    Series TV.
    Includes index.
    Summary: Describes how a television show is made, from
story idea through casting and filming to airing of the
finished show.
    1. Television — Production and direction — Juvenile
literature.    [1. Television — Production and direction.
2. Television programs]    I. James, Elizabeth.
II. Title.    III. Title: Series T.V.
PN1992.75.D7 1983      791.45'023      83-2119
ISBN 0-89919-142-8

P 10 9 8 7 6 5 4 3 2 1

# Acknowledgments

The authors wish to thank the following people and companies for their help with the manuscript: Cy Chermak and the production company of CHiPs; Judith A. Polone and ITC Productions, Inc.; Shirley Krims and The Burbank Studios, Technicolor-Vidtronics Division; Gary Coleman, Erik Estrada, Lara Jill Miller, and Adam Rich; Rosemary Abelson, Bill Barron, Gerry Colet, Jim Dunn, Kathi Fearn-Banks, Jimmy Giritlian and Ruxton, Ltd., Jim Miller, Alan Rafkin, Fred Silverman, Paul Stager, and Winifred White. Many thanks to Phil Stern for his photographs.

*For Francine and Cy,*
*and for David*

# Contents

# Series TV

# Introduction

Television is a powerful influence in people's lives. It reaches every country of the world. Children in Japan are aware of the California Highway Patrol because they watch *CHiPs*. A whole generation knows about the Korean War because of *M\*A\*S\*H*. And people all over the world know J.R. Ewing because of *Dallas*.

Television informs and entertains, but few people understand how the shows they watch came to be. The making of a show is as fascinating as the finished product. From the first page of the script to the finished show, this book offers an inside look at how an episode of a television series is made.

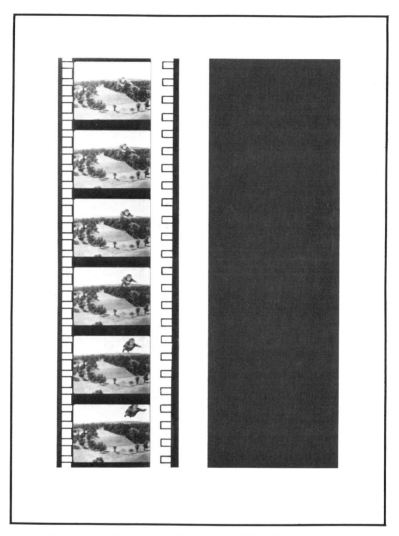

*Left:* This strip of developed 35-mm. film from an episode of *The Greatest American Hero* is really a series of six little pictures. Each picture is called a frame. The small square holes along the sides are called sprocket holes. They hold the film in place as it moves through the camera and projector. *Right:* Videotape looks and feels like a wider version of tape for a tape recorder, and it needs a video player to see what's on it.

# 1. The Starting Point

If you want to watch a certain television series show, but you can't remember what channel it's on, you don't have to look at a program guide to find out. All you have to do is turn on the set and listen. Each series has its own special theme music, and this music at the beginning of the show lets you know right away what you're watching. And even if hearing "Believe it or not, I'm walking on air . . ." doesn't ring a bell, seeing Ralph fly in his red jammies tells you *The Greatest American Hero* is about to start.

Each series has its own look and feel. The most obvious difference between series is whether shows are recorded on film or videotape.

The film used in television is the same 35-millimeter film that is used in making movies. That's why filmed TV shows look like short movies. Most dramatic series such as *Little House on the Prairie* and *Fantasy Island* are filmed. Action and adventure series like *The Dukes of Hazzard* and *The Greatest American Hero* are also filmed. They're shot outdoors as well as indoors, and each episode may be filmed in a different location.

Videotape was developed especially for television and is not yet used in movies. Taped shows look different from filmed shows. Just as a filmed TV show is similar to a movie, a taped show is like a play. Taped television looks "live," as if it were being performed as you watch. It's difficult to describe the visual difference between film and tape, but if you look at a show of each, you'll begin to see the contrast. Many situation comedies, also called "sitcoms," such as *One Day at a Time, Alice,* and *Diff'rent Strokes,* are taped while they are performed in television studios in front of an audience.

The decision to use tape or film is one way of giving a series its own look. Because taped shows take place indoors, you see Archie Bunker in his bar and not walking down the street. And because filmed dramas don't have live audiences, Tom Magnum on *Magnum, P.I.* won't get any applause for catching the crooks.

Setting and character are also important. Since *Little House on the Prairie* takes place in the late 1870s, Laura will never learn how to drive a car. And the Fonz probably will never hitch up a covered wagon. When Gary Coleman plays Arnold, he often puts his foot in his mouth. You can trust J.R. on *Dallas* to double-cross his brother, and George

Jefferson will certainly lose his temper at least once an episode.

The person responsible for the style of a show is the producer of the series. He oversees the making of every episode from beginning to end. He doesn't do this by himself, however. He heads a production company of more than one hundred people who work together to create each show.

One of the most important people on a series is the story editor. He or she, along with the producer, chooses the stories for each episode. A writer turns these stories into scripts.

Ideas for a story can come from anywhere, but they must be expanded. An episode needs a long and complicated story. Usually the producer, the story editor, and the writer meet for a story conference. Here they weave together several lines of thought to create an exciting plot. They bring fresh ideas for an episode that will work within the structure of the series.

A story conference for an episode of *CHiPs* might go like this:

WRITER: What if the main CHP computer shut down? Think of the mess it would cause — there'd be no way of tracing missing vehicles, they couldn't check drivers' licenses for tickets. . . .

PRODUCER: Not bad.

STORY EDITOR: And I can't remember doing a show with this idea.

PRODUCER (to writer): What's the story?

WRITER: I don't have it all worked out, but what if the "heavies" were guys who sabotage computers and steal computer parts?

STORY EDITOR: Maybe one of them could work with Ponch. He could be teaching him how the computer works.

PRODUCER: Better yet, this guy could be worried that somebody could sabotage the computer. So he does it himself to prove how easy it would be.

WRITER: Yeah! And he wouldn't really be a heavy. What if he had a buddy who was going to help him, but it turns out that the buddy is really a thief who steals computer parts.

PRODUCER: I think this story has possibilities.

STORY EDITOR: I think so, too. By the way, I just read in the newspaper that the navy is going to demolish an old airplane hangar. It would be really dramatic to film them blowing it up. Do you think you could work that into the story?

The meeting will go on until everyone feels confident that they have an intriguing one-hour story for CHiPs.

Now it's the writer's job to produce a story outline or treatment, which is a description of the plot and characters. She or he will rewrite this twenty-page treatment several times. The story editor makes sure that the written description of the story is right for the show and its characters. The stars must have

Producers work wherever the show needs them. Here Cy Chermak (*left*), executive producer of *CHiPs*, consults with Larry Wilcox, who plays Jon.

the most important roles, and they must stay in character. For example, in *CHiPs*, Ponch can never be the villain. The story treatment also can't contain a scene that's impractical to shoot. If the town of Malibu won't allow TV film crews there, a key scene set on Malibu pier needs to be changed. When everyone is satisfied that all the details make sense, the producer asks the writer to write a script.

The script, or screenplay, for a one-hour filmed television show like *CHiPs* runs fifty to sixty pages. It includes brief descriptions of the scenes, the actors' movements, and some directions for the camera. For instance, if one of the characters is supposed to be afraid, the script might suggest a close-up shot to capture the expression of fear on the actor's face. More important, the script contains the words, or dialogue, that each character says.

A script for a half-hour taped show such as *Diff'rent Strokes* usually runs forty to forty-five pages. It is written in a similar format, with the characters' names in the middle of the page and their dialogue underneath. But there are no camera directions. And there are practically no descriptions of

This is a page of the script from an episode of *CHiPs*. The scene numbers are typed in both the left and right margins so they are easy to spot. Dialogue is centered in the page, with the name of the character who says the lines above them in capitals. Scene headings are in capitals, and so are other directions like "chattering" and "whistles."

6.

25   IN THE ALLEY - THE WINO                          25

grabs his brown bag, uncorks it, takes a big swig.


26   EXT. ROOF OF BUILDING - A MONKEY                 26

has paused in F.G., PAN OFF TO what he sees: Jon and
Ponch coming over the edge, onto the roof.  They
separate a bit to approach the animal from different
angles.  Jon haunches down, extends a hand, softly
snaps his fingers -- and as they advance carefully:

                    JON
          C'mon, boy!  Here, boy!  Nice
          monk!  Nobody's gonna hurt you!
          ... Talk to 'im, Ponch.

                    PONCH
          You have the right to remain
          silent...

Simultaneously, Jon lunges and the Monkey makes a
break.  Jon goes flat.  Ponch gives chase.  Jon leaps
up and follows.


27   THE MONKEYS - (INTERCUT)                         27

The one that stopped joins the others, and they all
take off, moving in a predetermined general direction,
having a lot more fun than they anticipated.  They
scamper hither and thither, climbing, leaping, drop-
ping from obstacle to obstacle, roof to roof, always
just as far out of reach as they choose, CHATTERING
and mocking the CHiPs.


28   JON & PONCH (INTERCUT)                           28

are thrown into frustrated, stumbling confusion by the
minor moves of the little fugitives, but they manage
to keep them in sight and move in the same general
direction.  MEANTIME:


29   EXT. 2ND ALLEY BELOW - THE CANOPIED PICKUP TRUCK  29

hurries into position at the rear of the building.


29A  PICKUP TRUCK - CLOSE ANGLE                       29A

The cab door is opened by the driver, LOU POOLE, an
intense man of 30 in neat denims.  He WHISTLES.

7

                    ARNOLD

        Does this look like the face of a

        jiver?

(SMILES ANGELICALLY AT HER)

                        DOLORES

(LAUGHING)

        I can't resist those cheeks.

(PINCHES THEM)

                        ARNOLD

(AS SHE PINCHES)

        Can Dad come down and apologize?

        You're real special to him, Dolores.

        Please?  Please?  Put the poor guy

        out of his misery.

                        DOLORES

        Oh, all right.

                        ARNOLD

        Thanks!  Can I use your phone?  I'll

        call him at the office and tell him.

                        DOLORES

        Sure...

(INDICATES)

        Help yourself, honey.

(ARNOLD HOPS OUT OF CHAIR AND GOES

TO PHONE)

the scenes because taped television shows use the same sets over and over. Everyone knows what Bonnie Franklin's living room looks like on *One Day at a Time.*

The script goes through several changes before it is ready to be filmed or taped. When the writer finishes the first version of the script, the producer and story editor read it. Then the three of them discuss possible changes. Once they've all agreed, the writer rewrites those parts of the script. This is called a revision. The original script is typed on white paper. Each revision is done on a different color paper. Since only the revised pages are typed on a new color, a final script may look like a rainbow.

Some shows hire a different writer for each episode. The producers of these shows like the fresh approaches they get from a variety of writers. They know that the story editor will make sure each episode will fit into the series.

Other shows have a group of writers, headed by the story editor, who write every episode. The producers of these shows want their series to be almost like books with chapters instead of having totally

This is a page of the script from an episode of *Diff'rent Strokes.* Dialogue is centered on the page with the speaker's name on top in capitals, but there are very few stage directions (also in capitals and in parentheses). Scripts for taped television look a lot like scripts for plays.

different stories each episode. In these series, one character's problem may begin in one episode and not end until several episodes later. For example, millions of Americans impatiently watched *Dallas* for months, waiting to find out who shot J.R. Only the staff of writers who knew the outcome could create episodes that led to the solution.

On most filmed shows, once the final script is completed, the writer's work is done. He or she no longer has anything to do with that episode. Now it is the job of others to turn the words into action.

# 2. Planning the Show

It takes enormous effort to create an episode of a television series each week. What makes it difficult is that there is so much work to do in so little time. After the script is finished, filmed series have only seven days in which to plan the coming show. Taped shows have only four days for their preparations. A long-running series may require twenty-six episodes. That's like making twenty-six short movies or plays in a year.

The producer hires a director for each episode. The director is the creative leader for that episode. He not only guides the actions of the cast during production, he also helps with the planning of the show. His first job is to read the script.

The director and producer meet with the rest of the people who will be working on the show for a concept meeting. Its purpose is to go over the script and make sure that everyone understands the story.

A concept meeting could go something like this. A dozen or more people crowd into the producer's office, each ready to discuss his or her view of the story. The wardrobe master speaks up. When he read the script, he imagined the villain to be a rich, middle-aged man. But the director saw the villain as younger and poorer. Will he wear designer jeans, a three-piece suit, or scruffy Levi's? The person in charge of casting also needs a mental picture of the villain. She has to choose an actor with the right look for the part.

The script calls for a robbery to take place in a shopping mall, but the location manager says, "No mall is going to let us shoot during business hours. You know how it is — customers stand around and watch us instead of shopping. Can we use a set here at the studio instead?" The set designer shakes his head; building a set would be too expensive. The director suggests that they look for a set that's already been built for another show. The coffee and doughnuts standing by hint that this will be a long meeting.

Now the head of each department goes off to plan the part of the production he or she is responsible for. The casting director needs to find actors and actresses to match the parts in the script. Most episodes need other characters in addition to the regular characters in the series. The casting director chooses several actors who are right for each one of the parts. She asks them to come to the studio to try out for the role. Each actor gets a page or two of the script to study. When it's his turn, he reads his part for the casting director, the producer, and the director of the episode.

Even small parts are cast carefully. The director looks for someone who can give something special to the role. In an episode of *Diff'rent Strokes*, Arnold's father's girlfriend is a hairdresser. One scene takes place in her beauty parlor while she is setting a woman's hair. Even though the woman has only a few lines, her part is important. Her facial expressions as she overhears Arnold's father argue with his girlfriend make the scene even funnier.

Scripts often include scenes with groups of people who have no lines. These people are called "atmosphere," or "extras." They are the two men in the back booth in Mel's diner, the couple playing shuffleboard on the Love Boat, the unnamed students in *Fame*. These extras are hired from an agency to provide a live, moving background to scenes.

The wardrobe master chooses the clothes for everyone in the show. This includes shoes, belts, and jewelry. He tries very hard to make the clothes appropriate to the character. Luke and Bo on *The Dukes of Hazzard* wear western-style clothes. They wouldn't look like themselves if they dressed like characters on *Happy Days*. If a show has a modern-day setting, the wardrobe master shops in regular clothing stores that the characters themselves might shop in. For example, Ann Romano on *One Day at*

*a Time* isn't wealthy; she wouldn't buy her clothes in an exclusive boutique, so her wardrobe is selected from department stores.

Shows that take place in the past or in the future have a different problem. When *Star Trek* was filmed, Mr. Spock's costume didn't come from Sears. It had to be designed and made especially for the show. *Little House on the Prairie* also must have wardrobes created for it. On shows with a historical setting, an expert on that period helps the wardrobe master decide what the characters should wear. For example, on *Joanie Loves Chachi*, none of the characters can wear Nike running shoes; these sneakers weren't fashionable in 1962.

Every show wants its costumes to be accurate for the time and place, but sometimes details are changed because the real thing doesn't look quite right. For instance, real California Highway Patrolmen button their uniform shirts to the top and clip on bow ties. But the stars of *CHiPs* felt silly in bow ties, so the wardrobe department designed their shirts to be left open at the neck.

Sometimes real life takes a lesson from make-believe. The wardrobe master on *CHiPs* had a problem with the uniform shirts pulling across the front when the actors rode on motorcycles. He solved the

The man sitting in the alley isn't really a tramp. He's an "extra." He adds atmosphere to the alley scenes for an episode of *CHiPs.*

problem by sewing zippers down the fronts of the shirts. That way the buttons wouldn't strain and the shirts looked neat all the time. The California Highway Patrol thought that was a good idea, too. Now real officers' shirts are closed with zippers and the buttons are just decoration.

Television shows are shot either on location or on sets. When a show films on location, the production company goes to an actual place like the one described in the script. Since almost all TV series are made in Los Angeles, the location manager, along with the producer and director, drive around the L.A. area looking for spots that meet the needs of the script. They take photographs of locations that look promising. They will make a final decision later.

Location shooting helps to make a show look realistic. When Ponch cruises the freeway, he is on real Los Angeles roads. *The Love Boat* uses a real cruise ship, and parts of *Dallas* are shot at a real mansion in Texas. Location managers also look for indoor locations. The inside of a coffee shop may be needed for one episode. Renting a coffee shop for a day or two gives the show an accurate feel and is cheaper than constructing a set that looks like one. Many parts of Los Angeles are used over and over, and

Many movie studios have a whole department to make costumes and to alter store-bought clothes to fit the actors and actresses.

Unusual stunts done on location help make *CHiPs* exciting.

viewers who visit the city will probably see familiar scenery.

Sets are designed to look like real places. Outdoor sets are usually built on the part of a movie studio's land which is called the backlot. Bret Maverick's entire town of Sweetwater was built on the backlot of the Burbank Studios. And just a few hundred yards away is Hazzard County. Before it was downtown Hazzard, the town square was used in many movies. Of course, the signs on the storefronts have

This aerial shot shows the huge Burbank Studios, home of Columbia Pictures, Warner Bros., and also several smaller movie and television companies. Beyond the curved-roofed sound stages you can see the streets and buildings of the backlot. *Photo Credit: The Burbank Studios*

been painted to make you believe that this is really Boss Hogg's town.

Indoor sets are built inside large buildings called sound stages. If the interior of a particular building is going to be used in many episodes, the producer may decide to build an indoor set. The stationhouse on *Hill Street Blues,* the schoolrooms in *Fame,* and the operating room on *M*A*S*H* are all permanent indoor sets for filmed television shows.

Taped series use only indoor sets. Rooms that

It's easy to see how whole rooms could be built inside the sound stages lining this street at the Burbank Studios. *Photo Credit: The Burbank Studios*

The cast of *Fame* performs on the school cafeteria set.

appear on every episode, such as the house Nell works in on *Gimme a Break,* the living room on *Three's Company,* and the bar on *Archie Bunker's Place,* are permanent sets. Some of these sets have become so familiar that they are instantly recognizable. In fact, Archie's chair from the Bunker living room on *All in the Family* is now in the Smithsonian Institution.

Sets that are only used in one episode are called

The cast gets ready to tape an episode of *The Two of Us.* They stand on the set of the living room.

wild sets or swing sets and are built just for that episode. Since taped shows are confined to the indoors, it's important to give a feeling of movement to the episodes. One of the ways this is done is to put the characters in a new place. When Barbara and her boyfriend Mark on *One Day at a Time* go to Las Vegas, we can't see them getting there, but we can see them in the hotel's casino.

Art directors and set designers try to make their

sets as realistic as possible. A reporter would feel at home in the newsroom on *Lou Grant,* and the headquarters in *CHiPs* is an exact replica of the real Highway Patrol rooms in Sacramento.

Taped television shows are shot straight through from the beginning to the end. The scenes are taped in the same order they appear in the script, which is the order they'll be seen on TV. But filmed shows are not shot in order. Sometimes the last scene is filmed on the first day of shooting.

While each department works at its separate job, the unit production manager oversees and coordinates the planning of the show. For a filmed show, he decides the most practical order in which scenes should be shot. This is called the shooting schedule. For example, if part of a *CHiPs* episode takes place in downtown Los Angeles, it makes sense to film all the downtown scenes at once, even though they will appear in different spots in the finished episode.

Once the production manager is finished figuring out the shooting schedule, he asks the assistant director to prepare a cross plot board, which is simply called the "board." The information on its strips are used to plan each day's shooting. The strips on the board are movable so that if the shooting schedule changes, the board can be changed, too. If an actor gets sick or it rains on a day when an outdoor scene was planned, the shooting schedule will have to be changed.

A day or two before shooting begins, everyone gets

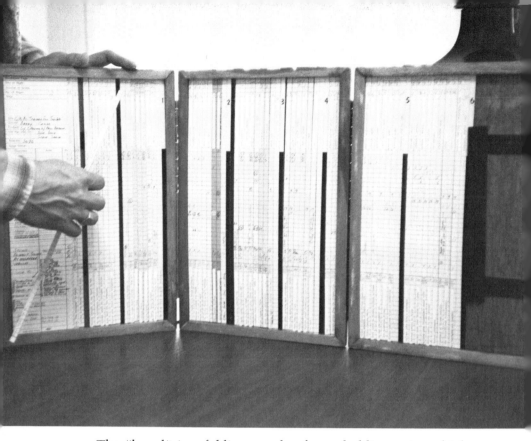

The "board" is a folding wooden frame holding strips which tell what scenes will be shot each day. Each strip tells the location of the scene, who is in it, and what special equipment is needed. The dark strips separate the days. The section on the far left lists all the actors and actresses, including extras, who will appear in the episode.

together again for a production meeting. Here the heads of departments discuss what they've been doing and the problems they've run into. On one show, chimpanzees and small monkeys are supposed to rob a bank. The propmaster says he has satchels for the monkeys to carry the stolen money in. But the animal trainer tells him that the satchels will be too heavy for the monkeys to carry. They finally decide to have the monkeys put the money

The producer, director, story editor, and heads of other departments for a filmed television episode sometimes hold their production meeting on an unused sound stage.

in the pockets of their overalls. The wardrobe master writes himself a note to make sure the overalls have large pockets. Before the meeting ends, most of the problems are solved.

The day before shooting is always hectic. Everyone is anxious for the show to begin and for no new problems to arise. The final version of the script is copied and given to everyone who will be working on the show. Since production begins the next day, everyone goes home to get a good night's sleep.

# 3. Laughter and Applause

Taped television shows are done in an incredibly short time. Once the script is complete and the cast is chosen, a half-hour sitcom is planned and produced in only five days.

On day one, the cast reads the script for the first time. The actors sit around a table with the director, producer, and story editor, and read their parts aloud. These early readings not only give the actors a chance to learn their lines, but also allow the director to hear how the script sounds. During these readings, everyone makes suggestions for changes so that the story becomes clearer and funnier. Lines sometimes sound odd when they are spoken. What looks humorous on the page may not draw a laugh when heard. Although the plot will stay the same, there will be many adjustments in the script over the next two days.

On the second day, rehearsals begin. The cast

members are still learning their lines, but now they are moving around while they speak. The director decides where and when the actors should sit and stand. A series episode would be boring if the actors just sat and talked to one another for a half-hour. Movement helps to tell the story, and it is as important for the actors to learn their movements as it is to learn their lines. For example, on *Alice,* if Mel's line is "I do all the work around here," it sounds true. But if he says the line as he leans against the counter while Alice struggles to carry a tray loaded with dirty dishes, the words take on a different meaning.

For the first three days, the cast practices in a rehearsal hall. This is a room large enough to be the size of the actual set. The real stage is being used to tape another show during these days. For example, *Diff'rent Strokes* and *Facts of Life* use the same sound stage.

At first glance the rehearsal hall looks like a regular room with some furniture in it. But the floor has long strips of colored tape on it. These tape lines show the actors where the walls and doors of the actual set will be. The furniture isn't the same as the audience will see when the show is taped. But similar pieces are used in the rehearsal hall to help the actors learn their places on the stage.

By the third day, most of the lines in the script are set. The actors know their parts and the movements they're supposed to make. Now they are

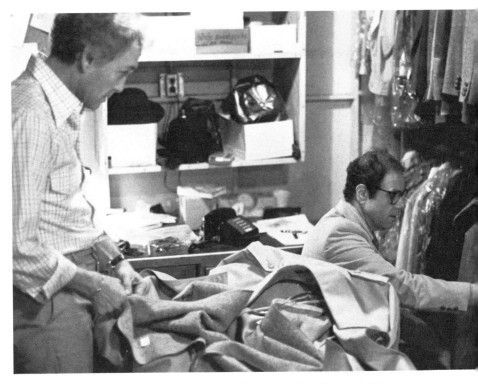

Oliver Clark (*right*), who plays Cubby on *The Two of Us*, discusses the wardrobe for his character with the wardrobe master.

ready to use props, which are small items such as silverware, dishes, or books used on stage during production.

On the fourth day, the director and cast move to the sound stage for rehearsals. The actors go through the episode several times. Some changes in their movements need to be made now that they are on the real set. And the cast wears the clothes that will

The lights above the set for this taped show are being adjusted.

be worn during the actual taping. This is called a dress rehearsal.

The fourth-day rehearsals are for the production crew as well as the cast. Lighting, sound, and camera crews need to see where the actors are when they say their lines. Much of the time during this rehearsal day is spent getting the production crew to work smoothly with the actors.

Four cameras are used to tape an episode. The camera operators roll these large modern cameras easily and silently across the floor. They raise and lower them hydraulically, much as a dentist raises and lowers his dentist's chair. All four cameras run throughout a taping. Each one tapes a slightly different view of the show.

Each view is called an angle, or shot. Every time the picture changes on the television screen, the angle has been changed. For example, on an episode of *The Jeffersons*, the audience sees a close shot of Mrs. Jefferson's face. Then the angle changes to show Mr. Jefferson coming into the room.

There are more than one hundred shots, or angle changes, in a half-hour sitcom. As the director reads through the script, he decides what angles he wants and where. He gives each camera operator a list of these shots so that during rehearsal the camera operators can practice their angles.

The fifth day of a taped television episode is the most exciting. It's the day when the actual taping is done. The cast goes to wardrobe and makeup, and the crew readies its technical equipment. But one important part of the production is missing — the audience. Taped television sitcoms are performed before live audiences. Laughter and applause encourage the cast, help the director know what jokes

These videotape cameras stand in front of empty audience seats, ready to be rolled toward the sets for shooting.

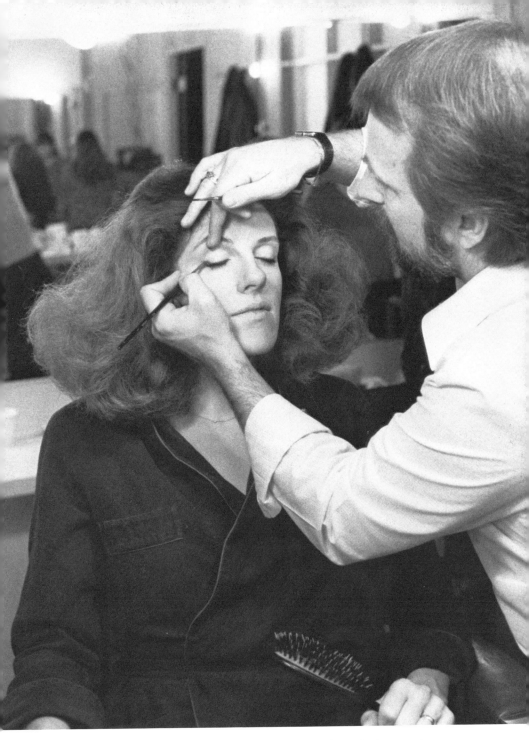

Each actor and actress must be carefully made up before taping.

work, and provide the sound track of audience response heard during the show.

Shows are so eager to have audiences that they give away approximately two hundred tickets for each of their tapings. There are two tapings for each episode, and each has a different audience. These tapings are usually separated by a lunch or dinner break for the cast and crew.

Even though a half-hour sitcom is only twenty-two minutes without commercials, each taping of the show takes slightly more than an hour. Some of the extra time is taken up with wardrobe changes. For example, in an episode of *One Day at a Time*, Barbara is supposed to wash her hair. In one scene it is wet, and in the next it is dry. Blow-drying her long hair required a ten-minute break between scenes. Also, actors sometimes make mistakes in their lines and the scene must be repeated.

The audience waits outside the studio for almost an hour before getting seated. When the people enter the sound stage, ushers who are called pages take them up to their seats, which look like bleachers. The tiers of seats are on a platform more than six feet above the stage. The audience looks down at the performance.

Once the audience is seated, a person comes out

Makeup needs to be freshened during taping because the hot lights often make actors and actresses perspire.

Through the rails next to the audience seats you can see television monitors and the applause sign hanging from a high crossbeam. Wires hanging down over the seats hold microphones which record the audience's laughter and applause.

to explain a little about the show and make the audience feel welcome. This "warmup person" points out the many microphones hanging over the seats. Because these microphones record audience laughter and applause, the warmup person encourages the audience to be vocal in responding to the show. He also asks them to applaud when the overhead signs reading APPLAUSE light up.

Large television sets also hang above and in front of the seats. These monitors show the episode as it's being taped. Even though the audience can see most of the action, sometimes the cameras get in the way and make it difficult to watch a scene. During these moments, people look at the monitors to see what's happening. When the show is ready to begin, the warmup person leaves, but he will return during scene changes. Since his job is to keep the audience enthusiastic and eager to see the show, he tells jokes, asks people where they're from, and answers questions about the show.

The seats take up only a part of the large sound stage, which is about 150 feet long and 100 feet wide. The walls and ceiling, which rises 50 feet above the floor, are covered with what looks like hundreds of mattresses. This padding soundproofs the building.

Facing the seats are the sets. Each set is a room with three walls and no ceiling. Above the place where the ceiling would be are rows of hot lights with bulbs of 500 to 10,000 watts in them. This amount of brightness is necessary because videotaping requires a lot of light.

The space where the fourth wall would be faces the audience. There is no fourth wall so that the

Many episodes of *The Two of Us* show Nan step outside her front door to meet someone or to say good-bye. This door and front porch are made to look as real as possible. When you watch the show, it's difficult to believe the actors aren't standing outside in the sunshine.

cameras can shoot from that viewpoint. The sets are next to one another like a row of shoeboxes lying on their sides. There are rarely more than four sets used for an episode of a sitcom, one or two permanent sets and a couple of wild ones. In a theater, when the scene changes, the curtain drops and the props and furniture are replaced. But in a television taping, there is no curtain, and the scene changes by simply moving to the next set. This saves time.

The sets are in the middle of the sound stage. Behind them is the backstage area. Here there are dressing rooms, rooms for wardrobe and makeup, and the "green room." This room, which isn't always green, is a comfortable place where actors can relax and have a cup of coffee while they wait to perform.

When the warmup person leaves, the lights go on over the sets, the cameras move into position, and the actors take their places. The stage manager, a man or woman who oversees the activity on stage, holds a small blackboard in front of one of the cameras and announces the scene number. This blackboard also has the scene and episode title written on it so that this piece of videotape can be identified later. Then the stage manager starts her countdown: "Five, four, three, two." In the beat of time when she would have said "one," the action begins.

The stage manager and the camera operators all wear headphones to hear the director's instructions. He is sitting out of sight up in a control room.

The director works closely with the cast and crew on stage until the tapings. Then he disappears into the control booth. Since he can't be in two places at once, he must depend upon the stage manager to carry out his instructions. But when there are seri-

This control room is quite elaborate, and the extra screens can be used to add in visual effects or to replay parts of tape already shot. The loudspeaker above the screen lets the people in the control room hear what's being said down on the set.

ous problems, his voice booms out over a loudspeaker to get everyone's attention.

The director is not alone in the control room. He works with a technical director, an assistant director, and a production assistant. They sit at a long desk covered with dials and buttons. In the wall in front of them is a row of four small TV screens.

Each screen is numbered to correspond with one of the four cameras on stage. Above the small screens is a larger one which is called the master screen. The small screens show what each of the cameras sees all the time, and the master screen shows which angle is being used at that moment. The picture on the master screen is the same as the one on the monitors the audience is watching.

Behind the control desk are tall director's chairs for the writers. They watch the taping carefully and may make suggestions for changes in the second taping. Sometimes a network executive sits in on the taping as well.

The people at the control desk work as hard as the cast and crew below them. Each person has a script marked with the director's shots in front of him, and each has a special job to do. The assistant director's job is to remind each camera operator as his shot comes up. He speaks quietly into a microphone that is connected to the headphones below and addresses each cameraman by number: "Ready three, shot seventy-three." This tells the operator of camera number three to get ready for the seventy-third shot of the episode.

The director decides the exact amount he wants the angle to change. Instead of telling them with words, he snaps his fingers for the angle change. As the director snaps his fingers, the technical director presses a button and the picture changes on the master screen. At the same time, the production

Each show has tickets printed for audience tapings. The back of the ticket warns people not to take cameras into the studio because taking pictures is not permitted.

assistant presses the button on her stopwatch and times the length of the shot. In most sitcoms this process is repeated more than 100 times in a taping, and in some sitcoms it's done more than 250 times.

The jobs in the control booth require quick reflexes and intense concentration. It may seem that the control booth would be full of tension, but in fact everyone is able to watch the show and laugh at the jokes. They are trying to see the episode for the first time through the audience's eyes.

Being at a taping is exciting. In addition to seeing television stars, you are able to watch a show being created. You feel like an insider and have a closer connection to the show when you view it at home. If you want to go to a taping, you can write for tickets. Address your request to the show at the network on which it appears.

Here's where to write for tickets to be in the audience of your favorite television show:

ABC
4151 Prospect Ave.
Los Angeles, CA 90027

CBS
7800 Beverly Blvd.
Los Angeles, CA 90036

NBC
3000 W. Alameda Ave.
Burbank, CA 91523

# 4. Rolling! Speed! Action!

Taping a half-hour sitcom takes only two hours, but filming a one-hour episode takes seven days. Film is also shot in bits and pieces, not in the order of the story. For these reasons you can see why filming a one-hour television episode is never done before an audience!

Videotaping is a new technology, but film has been used since the beginning of the century. The last major advance in filmmaking was the addition of sound to motion pictures fifty years ago. Film uses old-fashioned equipment and hasn't changed its production methods for years. Comparing a videotaped production with a film production is like putting a Ford Mustang next to a Model T. Filming is slower and more expensive, but despite these disadvantages, most television series are done in film.

The majority of filmed television shows are shot with one camera. But there are some half-hour sit-

In this episode of *CHiPs,* animals rob a bank. Here the crew crowds into the corner of an alley in downtown Los Angeles to film a chimp with his bag of money as he escapes by jumping into a waiting truck. Even on bright days, lights are needed to correct shadows.

coms, such as *Happy Days, Laverne and Shirley,* and *Joanie Loves Chachi,* that are filmed with three cameras. These shows are produced the same way as four-camera taping. They have a five-day schedule of rehearsals, use indoor sets only, and are shot on a stage from beginning to end in front of an audience on the final day. Filming these shows still takes longer than taping, however. For each episode, it takes twice as long to film two run-throughs as to tape them.

Much of filmed television is not shot at the studio

but on location. A location day begins when the sun rises. An early start is necessary to get an entire film crew gathered and all their equipment set up at the location site.

Shooting on location requires setting up a miniature movie studio near the spot where filming will take place. The cast needs a place to change clothes, so portable dressing rooms and bathrooms are brought. The makeup person and the hairdresser share a trailer. A truck the size of a moving van is filled with clothes for wardrobe. The stars have their own recreational vehicles in which to rest during the day. A huge equipment truck carries the camera and lights. Another truck is jammed full of props, sound equipment, and folding chairs for the director, stars, and script supervisor. A special truck hauls an electrical generator which powers the lights and camera.

Food and coffee are an important part of film production. People snack and drink coffee throughout the long shooting day. So the catering truck with its soft drinks, coffee, and doughnuts is a popular part of the equipment and is the first stop when people arrive in the early morning.

Even though the filming won't start until later that morning, the cast needs to show up early as well. While the crew sets up the equipment, the cast gets into costume and makeup. Actors don't wear makeup just to look better. They need it because the bright lights make everyone look pale.

Portable dressing rooms and bathrooms are part of every location shooting. These were hitched to large trucks and driven to a parking lot the production company rented for the day near the shooting site.

There is one trailer on location that is used by the makeup man and the hairdresser. This trailer is a fully equipped portable salon with mirrors, lights, shelves of cosmetics, hot curlers, and blow-dryers all ready and waiting for the actors and actresses.

Trucks of all shapes and sizes hold the equipment needed for shooting on location. Notice the bicycle, a favorite form of transportation on location as well as on studio lots.

This is the view of the camera that actors and actresses have. Behind the cameraman's head is the sign for 5th Street in downtown Los Angeles, where this part of an episode was filmed.

They even wear it on their hands and any place else where skin shows.

Anyone who watches location filming for the first time may be surprised to see so many people working. They'd be especially surprised to see a firefighter, a nurse, and police officers as part of the production crew. But these people are there because they are needed for safety. The firefighter makes sure that the film crew with its equipment doesn't set up hazards for the public. The nurse supplies first aid if, for example, an actress trips and twists her ankle. The police officers control vehicle and pedestrian traffic. A film company attracts attention. An empty sidewalk fills in minutes with cu-

While the company sets up to shoot in this coffee shop, the show's nurse bandages up a crew member's twisted ankle.

No matter where location shooting is done, a crowd always seems to gather. A police officer is needed to keep onlookers out of the shots.

rious passers-by. It's a police officer's job to keep observers from interfering with the production.

The first shot of the day for an episode of *CHiPs* is about to begin. In this scene, Bonnie and Ponch are going to come out of a coffee shop and will be dumbfounded to see a chimpanzee running by them on the sidewalk. Dozens of people, mostly men, stand not far from the camera. These are not on-lookers but members of the film crew. In addition to the director and actors, filming requires a four-man camera crew, people to adjust the lights, the sound man and his assistant, two assistant directors, and several people who move things around.

When everything is ready, the cameraman says, "Rolling," to indicate that film is now rolling through the camera. He's ready to start shooting. The sound man shouts, "Speed," announcing that his sound recorder is running at the right speed. Then the cameraman's assistant writes the scene and shot number on a clapboard. This is a small blackboard with a piece of wood hinged to its top. He holds the clapboard in front of the camera, says, "Scene thirty-two, Take one," and snaps the hinged wood down on the top of the board. The director calls, "Action."

Bonnie and Ponch step out of the coffee shop, the chimp runs by, and they stare after it. Then they turn to each other and shrug. The director calls, "Cut." The camera stops filming, and the sound man stops recording. Pleased with the short scene, the director says to the director of photography, "I liked that, Bob. How did it look to you?" The man behind the camera nods and the director says, "Good. That's a print." The first day of shooting has begun well.

The director now wants a close-up of Ponch and Bonnie as they react to the chimp. In this shot the

The information written on the clapboard identifies the piece of film to be shot. When the top of the clapper is snapped down, it makes a noise. Later the recording of this noise and the picture of the two pieces of wood coming together allow someone to synchronize the sound and picture.

chimp won't be seen; only Ponch and Bonnie's faces will be on screen. The actors remain where they are, but there are other adjustments to be made. The camera operator changes the lens of the camera. Two lights have to be moved. Even though it's a sunny day, lights are used in outdoor filming to soften shadows.

Once again the director shouts, "Action," and Ponch and Bonnie repeat their shrug. But this time the director isn't happy with the expressions on the actors' faces. "I'd like you to look a little more surprised," he tells Ponch. "Let's do it one more time."

The second "take" pleases everyone, and the director tells the cameraman to print it. Since it costs money to print film that's been shot, the director decides which shots are worth saving and printing. If he's uncertain about which take is best, several takes of the same scene are printed. Unlike tape, where the director can see what's been shot immediately, film must be developed before anyone can see the scene. The director won't know until the next day how the film footage really looks, and by then it's too late to do it over.

Each day the director and producer spend half an hour in a screening room viewing the film shot the day before. The scenes have been printed overnight by the lab and strung together out of sequence. These pieces of film, called "dailies," give the director some feeling of how the episode is going to look.

Back at the filming, the script supervisor sits on a tall folding chair placed where he can see everything that's happening. His copy of the script is in a special notebook with pockets for pencils and a stopwatch. Even though he doesn't say much, his job is important. He marks on his script each camera

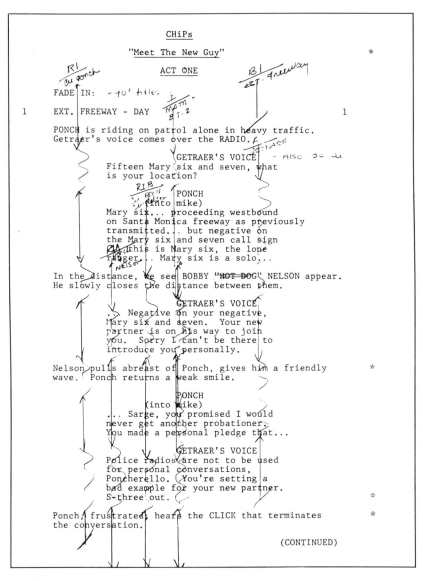

CHiPs

"Meet The New Guy"                                    *

ACT ONE

FADE IN:

1    EXT. FREEWAY - DAY                                      1

PONCH is riding on patrol alone in heavy traffic.
Getraer's voice comes over the RADIO.

                    GETRAER'S VOICE
          Fifteen Mary six and seven, what
          is your location?

                    PONCH
               (into mike)
          Mary six... proceeding westbound
          on Santa Monica freeway as previously
          transmitted... but negative on
          the Mary six and seven call sign
          ... this is Mary six, the lone
          ranger... Mary six is a solo...

In the distance, we see BOBBY "HOT DOG" NELSON appear.
He slowly closes the distance between them.

                    GETRAER'S VOICE
          ... Negative on your negative,
          Mary six and seven. Your new
          partner is on his way to join
          you. Sorry I can't be there to
          introduce you personally.

Nelson pulls abreast of Ponch, gives him a friendly       *
wave. Ponch returns a weak smile.

                    PONCH
               (into mike)
          ... Sarge, you promised I would
          never get another probationer.
          You made a personal pledge that...

                    GETRAER'S VOICE
          Police radios are not to be used
          for personal conversations,
          Poncherello. You're setting a
          bad example for your new partner.      *
          S-three out.

Ponch, frustrated, hears the CLICK that terminates         *
the conversation.

                              (CONTINUED)

The script supervisor's script is in a loose-leaf notebook so
that the pages lie flat. He draws lines down through the action
and dialogue to show which parts each take has recorded. The
back of the preceding page is used to explain in more detail.

angle that is shot and printed. He also times the length of each shot and keeps track of props and wardrobe. For example, if an actress is holding a cup of coffee in her right hand during one take, the script supervisor will remind her to pick it up in her right hand for the next angle as well.

The rest of the morning is taken up with more scenes outside the coffee shop. The cast and crew break for lunch at 12:30. Everyone walks a block to a parking lot where tables and chairs stand ready. Most of the people have been up since 5:00 in the morning, and they're very hungry. The caterers hired by the producer know that no one will be satisfied with peanut butter and jelly sandwiches. They offer a choice of three hearty meals from the kitchen in their catering truck. Roast beef, chicken, or fish comes with mashed potatoes, gravy, and two vegetables. In addition, there is a table of salads and fruits for dieting actors. Most actors have to watch their weight, because the camera makes them look ten pounds heavier.

The lunch break is short, usually less than an hour. After lunch, the *CHiPs* company goes to a new location spot — the inside of the coffee shop. The equipment is set up again. Electrical cables snake across the floor of the coffee shop, lights stand on tripods, the room fills with people. The director discusses the scene with the cameraman. Ponch and Bonnie are going to sit across from each other and talk while they have a cup of coffee.

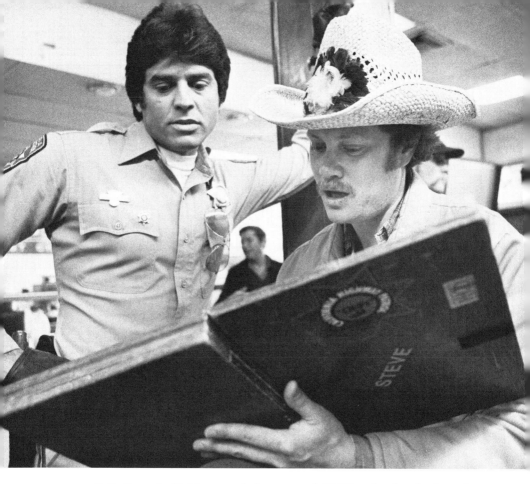

Erik Estrada (*left*), one of the stars of *CHiPs*, checks the board with the assistant director between scenes to see what's coming up next.

At the table, instead of Ponch and Bonnie, sit another man and woman about their same size. These people are stand-ins, and their job is to take the actors' places while the lights and camera are being prepared for the shot. The camera operator and lighting director need subjects in order to focus the camera and light the set. These adjustments take time, and the waiting would tire the actors. Besides, the actors are busy. Their makeup has to be freshened, their hair needs recombing, and they must learn their lines for the coming scene.

The only rehearsal in film takes place just before the scene is shot. Actors who only appear in a few scenes don't even get an entire script; they get copies of the pages on which their lines appear. The regular actors on the show get scripts which they read, but they don't usually memorize their lines until just before a scene is shot. Scenes are not filmed in the order of the story as they are in videotape. For instance, the opening scene may not be shot until the last day, and it's too confusing to memorize a long part out of sequence. There is enough time between shots to learn lines.

The cameraman tells the director they are ready to start. The camera is behind and to one side of where Ponch will sit, focusing on Bonnie's face. The sound man's assistant holds a long pole that has a microphone attached to the end of it. He hangs this boom microphone over the table and higher than the stand-ins' heads.

Bonnie and Ponch take their places at the table. The cameraman checks to make sure the microphone can't be seen through the camera, and Bonnie says a few words so the sound man can be sure he hears her through the microphone. The camera rolls, and Bonnie and Ponch speak their lines.

They do two takes. In the first one, halfway

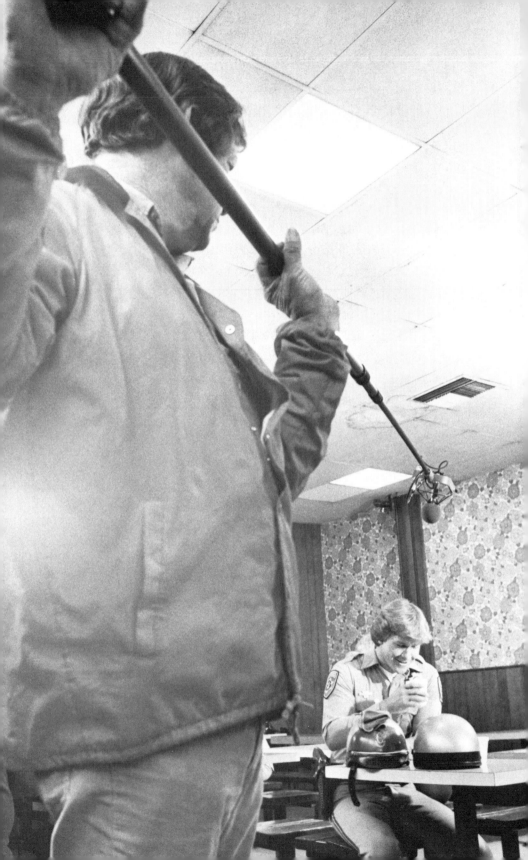

through Bonnie's speech, the cameraman called, "Cut. We're out of film." The cameras used in film production can only hold ten minutes' worth of film at one time. When that runs out, the cameraman puts in a magazine of fresh film. The second take, however, is fine.

Since the camera has photographed only Bonnie's face in the scene, it moves around to the other side of the table to shoot Ponch's face. Once more the lights have to be moved and the camera focused. Bonnie and Ponch do the scene again.

Shooting a scene with one camera takes a long time. But the advantage of having one camera and moving it is that it can photograph in every direction. By using one camera, each of the four walls of the coffee shop can be filmed. This gives the scene a realistic look.

Videotaped shows look flatter than filmed ones because in tape the "fourth wall" is never seen. It can't be seen because that's where the cameras are. In *All in the Family*, for example, Edith can watch Archie going upstairs, but the camera never shows Archie's view of looking down at Edith.

After the coffee-shop scenes have been shot, the production company moves to a nearby alley, which is the new location. The scene calls for Ponch and

The boom man holds the microphone over the actor's head high enough so that it's not seen in the picture but low enough so that the actor's voice can be heard.

Shooting *Fame* with one camera lets the director choose shots in almost any direction.

Jon to climb up an old outside fire-escape ladder after the chimpanzee.

Most people know that the stars of a show don't actually do dangerous stunts. The Duke boys aren't really in the General Lee car whenever it crashes. These stunts are done with doubles who are trained to perform dangerous feats. Usually the doubles are chosen for their resemblance to the stars as well as for their special abilities.

But car crashes aren't the only stunts that require doubles. This scene in the alley is potentially hazardous to Ponch and Jon. Chasing a chimp up the slippery iron rungs of a ladder might result in a sprained ankle or a fall. The stars are needed to film the rest of this episode and the ones following. It would be foolish to risk their safety when stuntmen can make the climb without danger.

The stuntmen wear clothes identical to Ponch's and Jon's. From the back they look the same as the actors they're doubling. The illusion that Ponch and Jon are climbing the ladder is created by shooting their faces while they stand at the bottom of the ladder and at the top. Then the doubles' backs are filmed as they climb up.

*The Dukes of Hazzard* creates the same kind of illusion when Luke and Bo are filmed driving the General Lee. The camera films their faces as they sit in the front seat. The next shot shows the car careening along a road so that the viewer imagines the boys are driving, but in fact they are not.

The dark-haired man with his back to the camera looks like Ponch on *CHiPs*. But he's really Erik Estrada's stunt double.

At last the long day of *CHiPs* shooting is over. The director calls, "It's a wrap." After a twelve-hour day it is time to wrap up the equipment and go home. With luck, they have managed to film enough footage to create just seven minutes of the forty-eight-minute episode.

Filming in a movie studio, whether on the backlot or in a sound stage, takes a long time, too. Even though the equipment is all nearby, people still have to arrive early. The cast needs to get into wardrobe and be made up. The lights and camera equipment need to be set up and adjusted. The sets need finishing touches. Still, it is easier to shoot in a studio than on location.

Sets for filming are constructed inside the same kind of sound stages as sets for taping. But there is no place for people to sit, since filming is not done before an audience. Instead of being lined up like a string of shoeboxes, all facing one direction, sets for filming are arranged together like real rooms would be. This way the camera can be in one room and catch glimpses of another room or hallway through an open door. Walking through the *Dallas* set is like being in a real house, and being inside the school set for *Fame* makes you feel as though you should get out your books and start studying. That is, until you look up.

Most sets have no ceilings. The illusion of a ceiling being there is created by dangling lights or chandeliers into the room, or set, from rafters high at the

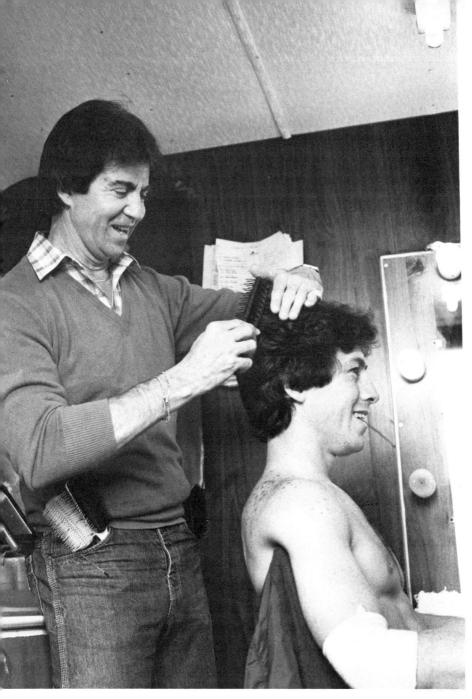

Hairdressing, makeup, and wardrobe are the beginnings of every actor's and actress's working day.

Movie studios have shops to make almost anything needed for a film or television show. *Photo Credit: The Burbank Studios*

top of the sound stage. Most people think that rooms have ceilings whether they see them or not. So the camera aims slightly above head height and catches glimpses of the hanging chandeliers in some of the shots.

The open tops of sets serve a purpose. Catwalks high on the crossbeams of the sound stage are designed to hold lights that can shine down through the open ceiling onto the set. Lighting men perch

Once walls, doors, furniture, and knicknacks are used in one show, they are stored so they can become part of the set for another show in the future. *Photo Credit: The Burbank Studios*

behind their huge lights thirty feet above the ground. Sometimes the sound man's assistant stands on the catwalk as well to direct his microphone down at the actors.

Some shows, such as *Fantasy Island* and *M\*A\*S\*H* use a backlot for exterior shooting. The advantage of this is that, like the sound stage set, the backlot set is permanent and requires less preparation than location shooting. Not only is the equipment nearby, but there are no crowds of onlookers because people are not allowed inside movie studios without permission.

Another reason for using a backlot is that sometimes it is difficult to find the proper setting on location. Where would the production company find a location for the Korean War's M*A*S*H unit in today's world? Even if it were possible to find a real place to shoot *Fantasy Island*, it would cost a fortune and take too much time to shift an entire film crew there week after week. Besides, the set designers have made part of the backlot of the Burbank Studios look just like a tropical island.

Outdoor sets are expensive to build and maintain, however. *Hawaii Five-O* used indoor and outdoor

Large movie studios have at least one "western street" where the fronts of the buildings can be changed to fit the show that's being shot there. *Photo Credit: The Burbank Studios*

Most television series shows are filmed either on location around Los Angeles or inside a movie studio. Boss Hogg's town on *The Dukes of Hazzard* is really part of the Burbank Studio's backlot behind these studio walls.

sets built especially for the show in Hawaii. After the show left the air, *Magnum, P.I.* was created to take advantage of these facilities. For six months a year the cast and crew of this show live in Hawaii.

Whether a show is filmed on location or at the studio, it's still a complicated process. Lights must be shifted for each shot, the camera must be moved, and the actors must repeat the scene for each camera angle. In addition, the scenes are shot out of order no matter where the filming takes place.

Because it takes so much longer to film a show than to tape one, filming costs more money. Yet many people feel the final product is worth it.

# 5. Making Magic

A large group of people work on the planning and production of both taped and filmed shows. But that's not the end of the job. While the production team goes on to creating the next episode, a whole new team of people begin to work on the episode that's already been shot. This part of getting a show ready to go on the air is called post-production.

When you watch a show on television, you see only the cast of characters. The rest of the people involved in making the show remain behind the scenes. Only their names appear on the show. The lists of job titles and names at the beginning and end of a show are called the credits. Most people who watch television don't pay much attention to the credits, but if you know what these jobs are, the credits become an interesting part of the show.

More than twenty people work on the post-production of a filmed episode. Even though the

producer is responsible for the whole show, the person who is in charge of this phase is the post-production supervisor. He oversees the editing, scoring, dubbing, and looping that turn the film footage into a finished episode.

A film editor works in a room that's just large enough to hold him, his equipment, and the film. Of the 12,000 feet of film that have been shot and printed, he must choose approximately 4,300 feet of film for the one-hour television episode. He's already come up with some ideas of what shots he'll put together to make up a scene while watching the dailies during the week of filming. And he has rolled up each group of film takes and marked them.

Now he has the script supervisor's script full of notes in front of him, and the little rolls of film sit in racks above his workbench. Taking the first shot of a scene, the editor runs the film through his Moviola, a machine used to view 35-millimeter film. The film moves through this machine at projector speed. The Moviola lights and magnifies the film image so that the editor can watch the action on a 3-inch-by-4-inch window on top. Although a Moviola is powered by electricity, the editor operates it with a foot pedal and can make the film move very slowly if he likes.

For each scene, there are several camera shots or angles. The editor discusses with the show's producer and director how they want the scene to look. On *Hill Street Blues*, for example, here is the footage

the editor might be looking at. In this scene, Joyce Davenport walks into Captain Furillo's office with a complaint. She tells Furillo that she thinks one of his officers roughed up one of her clients. Furillo disagrees. She storms out the door. The editor has three pieces of film. One of them is the whole scene with all the dialogue, but all that is seen is Frank's face. Another angle is the whole scene again, but this time with Joyce's face on the screen. The third piece of film is a two-shot, which is the entire scene with both actors on screen talking to each other.

The editor uses the two-shot for most of the scene. But on Joyce's last line, when she tells Furillo off, he decides to use the close-up of her. Then he will end the scene with the close-up of Furillo's face watching as Joyce angrily leaves his office.

The editor then cuts the pieces of film and tapes them together until he has one piece of film with the scene on it. He does this by marking each shot, with a wax pencil, at the point he wants it to start and to stop. Then he takes the film out of the Moviola and puts it down on his workbench. Using a tool called a butt splicer, he cuts out the piece he wants. He joins the end of this piece to the beginning of the next piece with special clear tape. Once

This editor is splicing film together at his workbench. In the left foreground of the photo is the back of his Moviola with its cloth bin for catching the film as it runs through the machine.

75

The butt splicer is in the center right of the photo; its sharp blade faces the editor's hand. He pulls down on the flat, round top of the blade to slice the film between frames. You can see the film with its individual frames on the left. On the right is the sound track that was recorded during filming. The quarter-inch sound tape is put on clear 35-mm. celluloid, and another strip of blank tape is added to the other edge to balance the weight.

he has edited each scene, he tapes all the scenes together in the order of the story. Then he shows it to the producer of the show. When it is approved, the editor turns the film, which is five reels long, over to the lab.

The film that the editor gives to the lab is called the work print. The lab or optical house makes three black-and-white copies of this print. One copy goes to the music editor, one to the sound-effects editor, and the third to the looping editor. While these departments use these black-and-white prints for their work, the lab cuts the original negative to match the work print. Once the sound and music have been added to it, this negative will be used to make the final copy shown on television.

While the film editor pieces together the film, the composer and sound editor talk about what kind of music this episode needs and where it should go. This is called scoring. In addition to theme music at the beginning and end of the show, each filmed episode has music created for it. After looking at the script, the composer writes music that fits the story and action.

Background music sets the mood and tone of the show. A scary or sad scene is heightened by the music. The producer also wants the music to appeal to the show's audience. *Joanie Loves Chachi*, which has a young audience, uses music with a rock beat.

Every note of music heard on a filmed episode has been played by an orchestra just for that episode. Scoring is done in a large, soundproofed room. There are seats for about twenty musicians, and the conductor stands on a platform so the musicians can see him. High on one wall is a large movie screen.

A soundproofed window separates the scoring room from the control room. Here the sound engineers work with panels of buttons and dials that adjust levels of tone and sound. There are also large

Television production companies rent music recording studios when they score their shows. This recording studio, or scoring stage, is at the Burbank Studios. *Photo Credit: The Burbank Studios*

speakers in the control room so that the editors can hear the music.

When a scoring session begins, the musicians and the conductor take their places in the scoring room. The sound engineers watch the musicians and the movie screen through the window. The screen will show the episode to be scored. It's very important that the music begin and end at exactly the right points in the film, so a sound editor marks his copy of the film to show these points. The musicians can see these marks while the film is run. In addition, each musician wears earphones that play a "click track," which is a timed series of clicks that help musicians start at the right place.

All sound that isn't music or dialogue is the responsibility of the sound-effects editor. Just as music is added during a scoring session, the sound effects are blended during a dubbing or mixing session. When the film was shot, many sounds besides the dialogue were recorded. Footsteps, a door closing, a motorcycle revving — these are all sounds that the sound man may have recorded during shooting. But sometimes these sounds aren't loud enough. Other noises, such as rain or ducks quacking, may not have been part of the shooting.

The sound-effects editor has a library of extraordinary sounds on tape. They range from a cat's meow to a gargoyle's scream. The library also includes more common noises such as a clock ticking, a boat creaking, glass breaking, and crickets chirping. He adds sounds to the film to make it more realistic and to give a feeling to a scene.

Sounds already on the film that are too soft need to be made louder, or "sweetened." A scene in which a character is pushed into a lake doesn't sound right without a big splash. So the sound-effects editor looks into his library for a loud splash sound. And sounds not on the film may need to be added. When the scene was shot, there were ducks on the lake, but they didn't make any noise when the actor fell in. The editor adds duck quacks and mixes it with the splash to make the sound more natural.

Like the control room during the scoring session, the dubbing room is full of electronic equipment. The sound mixers sit behind a panel of dials and knobs and watch the episode on a big screen in front of them. Once the sounds are all in place and the volumes are right, the entire sound-effects track is "locked in" and recorded. This tape or track is now ready to be added to the final film.

Looping is re-recording an actor's lines in a looping studio. Sometimes an actor mumbles his lines or a background noise, such as a rumbling truck, makes his speech impossible to be heard. That dialogue needs to be looped. The actor comes to the studio and watches himself say the lines on a screen. He practices repeating the lines the way they should be said, using a digital counter under the screen to help him begin at the right point. Because this process is time-consuming, series television's tight schedule doesn't allow for much looping.

Sometimes a television series uses special effects. The Starship Enterprise on *Star Trek* isn't really out in space, and the Greatest American Hero's suit

The sound effects engineer watches the show on a large screen in front of him so that he can make the sounds and noises fit the picture.

docsn't actually make him fly. Special effects in post-production create these illusions. This is the one part of filmmaking that takes advantage of the most up-to-date computerized equipment.

A process called blue screen or green screen is used in many flying special effects. *The Greatest American Hero* works with blue screen. Ralph wears a harness under his red suit and is suspended in a room that is covered with blue fabric. The cable that holds him up is also blue. The camera films him in a variety of flying angles. At some other time the special-effects director shoots background footage. Sometimes this is shot from a crane or helicopter to get Ralph's point of view when he looks down. A machine called the Ultimatte puts the background footage everywhere blue appears on foreground footage.

In the same way, a van can "fly." The real van is not suspended, but a miniature is. And when the closer shots of the van full of people are taken, the blue background curtain is used. Since the Ultimatte puts background footage everywhere blue appears, none of the costumes or props can be blue in these scenes. A green screen works the same way, but all the backgrounds are green instead of blue.

Post-production in videotape is much faster than in film. This is because most of the editing takes place during the actual taping. The director chooses his angles before shooting, and since he can see these tape angles while they're being shot, he edits the tape on the spot.

An orchestra is only needed once to play the show's theme music. This is done for the first show of the series. The theme is recorded and played for the following episodes. Music other than the theme music is rarely used in taped television, and when it is, it is also prerecorded. This makes the music editor's job faster and easier.

Post-production of a taped episode takes just two or three days. The editor takes the best parts of the two tapings and combines them electronically. He makes sure that the final taped version won't run over thirty minutes, including commercials. Even though the director watches the timing closely, the editor may need to shorten a scene.

Mixing is simpler in tape, because the editor uses the sounds that are recorded during the tapings. But sometimes the laughter and applause from the audience aren't enthusiastic enough, so the editor "sweetens" the audience's response by increasing the volume.

One of the things that makes tape production fun is that the equipment allows the editor to perform "magic" on the screen. He can put one scene on half a screen and another scene on the other half at the touch of a button. Or he can insert a person doing sign language for the deaf at the bottom of the screen. It takes just seconds to divide the screen

This videotape editing bay shows the complicated switching panels that videotape editors use to create "magic." *Photo Credit: Technicolor-Vidtronics Division*

into little boxes showing a variety of scenes.

In film, dissolves (in which one scene melts into another) and fades (in which one scene fades out and another fades in) must be done at an optical house.

But in tape, the editor can create these scene changes instantly. Because tape is a new medium, it's designed to use the latest computerized technology. Its speed, economy, and versatility intrigue many television producers. For these reasons, more and more television shows are being produced on tape.

Erik Estrada

# 6. An Actor's Life

Being a successful actor or actress is often glamorous and exciting. People recognize stars when they walk down the street, stars are interviewed and asked their opinions on many subjects, and they earn good salaries. In addition, actors and actresses are doing the work they love best.

An actor's life, however, is not all fun. Acting in a television series requires long hours and hard work. And that's only for the people lucky enough to have a role in an episode. Much of an actor's time is spent trying out for parts. Unfortunately, there are many more actors than there are parts, so actors must get used to the disappointment of rejection. Regulars on series usually have jobs as long as the show runs. But once the series ends, they also must look for new roles. Even famous actors don't get all the parts they try out for.

Being famous has drawbacks. When an actor or

*Fame* is a series that shows the work and struggle that is part of becoming a performer.

actress is first stopped for autographs, he or she finds the attention flattering. But many stars can't go to stores or restaurants without being hounded by fans. They don't like giving up their privacy, but if people stop being interested in them, they worry that their careers are in danger. It's also difficult for an actor to know whether someone who is friendly genuinely likes him or whether that person simply likes being close to someone famous. Erik Estrada says, "I don't know who my friends are."

Another inconvenience of being a performer is having to look good all the time. Many actors and actresses take exercise classes, and most watch what they eat. There is rarely much advance notice for a casting appointment; the actor doesn't have time to quickly diet and get in shape for the interview.

Child actors may not have the problems of dieting and getting enough exercise, but their changing appearance as they grow creates a different kind of problem. When Adam Rich began *Eight Is Enough*, he was ten years old. Like many child stars, he looks younger than his age and could play the part of an eight-year-old. Adam still looks young for his age, but eventually he will need to look for teenage and young adult parts.

Some shows allow their child stars to "grow up" during the series. From her beginning as young Laura Ingalls on *Little House on the Prairie*, Melissa Gilbert has grown into a woman and has even gotten married on the series. When *One Day at a Time* began in 1975, Valerie Bertinelli played fifteen-year-old Barbara Cooper. Now Valerie is a married woman in real life, and her character on the series is engaged. But if a series doesn't run long enough to make these changes work for the characters, young actors and actresses have to look for new and different types of parts.

There are other problems that especially affect child actors. Most children don't work for a living. While adults only have to work during the day, a

Adam Rich

child actor must squeeze both work and growing up into his or her life. It's hard to get together with friends when the studio day is so long. And a young performer can't get to baseball or soccer practice if it conflicts with the shooting schedule.

In addition to work, young actors and actresses must also go to school. California has a law requiring child performers to attend three hours of school each day they are working. Screen Actors Guild, the union to which all professional movie and television actors belong, also has strict rules about school and working conditions for young actors. For instance, a period of less than twenty minutes of teaching doesn't count as school time. These children don't have classes in a regular school, however. School is brought to them. They may have their classes in a trailer, a rehearsal room, or even in a vacant lot on location.

Studio teachers are licensed teachers who work in the entertainment industry instead of in regular schools. They can teach children from first grade through high school, and they can teach all subjects. Any television show that hires child actors has to provide a teacher on the set. *Archie Bunker's Place* has only one school-age performer, Danielle Brisebois, and one teacher serves as her tutor all season. Even if there are several children on a series, one teacher usually teaches all of them. One episode of *Diff'rent Strokes* was about a birthday party for Arnold. Even though the children at the party only worked the one week the episode was shot, they still had to go to school on the set. And one teacher taught them all.

Gary Coleman

How can one teacher work with a group of children of different ages and from different schools? First of all, the child actors don't waste time; they are there to learn quickly. Second, each child brings books and assignments from his regular school so he can keep up with his class. Still, the teacher has a difficult job, because he or she may have to teach as many as sixty subjects in three hours.

Most child actors are bright and catch on quickly. Memorizing lines and stage moves is as difficult as learning multiplication tables and spelling words. For children who miss only a few days of school, falling behind isn't usually a problem. A youngster who has a regular role in a series, however, gets ninety percent of his education from the studio teacher. If he doesn't take these classes seriously, he will have problems in regular school once the series stops shooting.

Being the only student in class may sound appealing. But there's no one else for the teacher to call on; that means one student has to be prepared all the time. Being the only student also can be lonely. There's no one across the aisle to joke with. In fact, there's little chance for any socializing in a day that includes three hours of school, one hour of recreation, four hours of work, and lunch.

The glamour of being a child actor is so attractive that other kids often wish they were actors, too. They may think that wearing makeup is great, but they don't realize that sitting in a chair for an hour

Lara Jill Miller

and a half having makeup applied to their arms and legs as well as their faces would be boring. They probably think that getting fan mail is neat but don't consider the hours it takes to answer it. They imagine that life in Los Angeles is full of excitement but don't stop to think that the series actor is too busy working to go sightseeing.

Resentment and envy are two problems child stars must cope with. Lara Jill Miller, who plays Samantha on *Gimme a Break*, says, "It's hard for me when I go home to Pennsylvania. I have one good friend, but other kids in my high school think I'm stuck up."

With all these problems, why would any kid want to work so hard to be a star? One reason is that they are paid well. Even though much of a child actor's salary is saved for his adulthood, there is still enough money left for expensive toys and other luxuries. Adam Rich, from *Eight Is Enough* and *Code Red*, says he likes earning a good salary. "I can buy a lot of things and I can go to interesting places." But the best part of being a child star is being able to act. As much as they would like to be home playing with their friends, they feel the sacrifice is worth it because they love their work.

# 7. A Matter of Choice

So far this book has described how a television show is created and produced. But how does a show get on the air? A production company makes a show and owns it. Then the production company rents the show to television. A network such as NBC, CBS, or ABC pays the production company for the right to broadcast the show on television. It pays for this right because it will then sell commercial time to sponsors.

A sponsor buys commercial time because it wants to sell its products to you, the viewer. If Procter and Gamble sponsors *The Dukes of Hazzard*, when you watch the show you also may have to watch a commercial telling you how to get your teeth brighter (unless you go to the refrigerator during the break). Since the networks charge advertisers so much money to sponsor a show, several companies buy that time. Almost one-quarter of the show time is used to sell you everything from dog food to cars.

The networks and the sponsors determine what is aired on commercial television. They look for shows that lots of people want to see. More people watching the show means more people watching the commercials and perhaps buying the products. But no one knows which new series will turn out to be popular. When production companies come to the networks with their series ideas, the networks can only guess whether viewers will like these shows. The public's taste is impossible to predict, and network executives sometimes lose their jobs when they guess wrong.

Once a show is on the air, the number of viewers it attracts can be measured. The best-known way of measuring popularity is the Neilsen rating system. The A. C. Neilsen Company selects several hundred families that it feels represent the whole viewing audience. Some of these families have little boxes attached to their television sets to record which shows are watched. Others fill out weekly reports describing their viewing habits. Those shows which are most watched that week get the highest ratings.

Every Tuesday, people who work in television anxiously await the results of the Neilsen ratings. And so do the sponsors. There are 81.5 million households in the United States that have television sets, and Neilsen rates approximately seventy shows each week. This is more than an interesting contest. The survival of a show depends on these ratings. A show that doesn't stay in the top third of the ratings is likely to be canceled.

It may seem that you, as an individual viewer, don't have any say in what programs stay on the air. But sponsors care what you think. They sponsor shows because they want people to buy their products. If people write to the sponsor of a show, the sponsor pays attention. If enough people praise a show or complain about it, the sponsor may respond by keeping the show on the air or getting it canceled.

Since sponsors care about audience opinion, it pays to be a critical viewer. Watching television is entertaining, but it's more fun if you can compare and evaluate what makes one show better than another. Television is like a supermarket. Just as there are lots of kinds of detergents to choose from, there are many shows on television. The more you know about TV, the better you are able to make your choice.

By now you know how shows are made and what helps to make them entertaining. But there are other things to look for besides production technique. Believability is an important part of a good show. Do the children on different television shows seem like real kids? Another question you could ask yourself is whether a show needs so much violence to be entertaining. You already recognize shootings, brawls, and car crashes as acts of violence. But there are other ways to hurt people, like hurled insults and verbal put-downs. You may not have noticed some of this hostile behavior because much of it is supposed to be funny. Once you start looking at television more closely, you'll see that a show reveals more than simply the story. At the end of this chapter is a checklist to help you rate programs yourself.

Even after you've decided which are the best shows on television, there is something else to consider — the amount of television you choose to watch. Television has much to offer. It's relaxing and entertaining. It can teach you things and take you to new places. Television is not real life, however.

When you watch someone on television walk along the ocean's edge, it may look great. But it's not the same as being there yourself. You won't smell the salt air and feel the sand between your toes by watching it on TV. When you're watching television, you're watching other people doing things instead of doing things yourself. You can't be in two places at once. If you're in front of the set, you can't be outside playing soccer at the same time.

What you know about how television shows are made will make you a more active viewer. While you're watching TV, ask yourself if you're really enjoying the show. Is it funny? Instructive? Exciting? Or is it insulting? Boring? Dumb? Be selective in choosing which shows you watch, and let sponsors know how you feel. It's a matter of choice, and it's up to you to choose.

# 8. A Rating Index

For each show, use a scale from 1 to 5 as you answer the questions below. Give it a 1 for the worst rating and a 5 for the best. Use a separate sheet of paper — don't write in the book.

## The Look of the Show

- If the show is taped, how do you like its overall look?
- If it's filmed, how do you like its overall look?
- If the show was shot in a studio, how do the sets look?
- If it was shot on location, are the location choices good?
- If it was shot both in a studio and on location, do you like how much was done of each?

- Do the actors look right for their parts?
- Do the costumes seem appropriate for the show?
- Do the stunts, like car crashes, seem real?
- Do the special effects, like flying, look real?
- If people are riding in cars, does it look like they're actually moving?
- Was the crew careful to keep technical equipment, such as microphones, out of the picture?
- Did the director do a good job with the pace and look of the show?
- Do the commercials fit into the show's format?
- Are there too many commercials? (Give a lower rating if you feel bombarded by commercials.)

## The Sound of the Show

- Does the story make sense?
- Does the story seem possible?
- Is the story fresh and different from other stories used in the series?
- Does the music fit the action and mood of the show?
- Does the laughter on a sitcom come at the right times?
- Does the overall volume of the show seem appropriate?
- Are the commercials the same volume as the show?

## The Messages in the Show

- How real do the children on the show seem?
- How real do the adults on the show seem?
- After seeing the show, do you wish you could be like the people on it?
- Are members of special groups, like old people, women, and minorities, portrayed with respect and as individuals?
- Does the show avoid sexually suggestive clothing and comments?
- Does the show avoid violence that is unnecessary to the story?
- If the show idealizes life, is it clear that not everyone needs to live that way?

## How Does This Show Rate?

Add up the points you gave for each question, and then use the scale below to rate the show.

- 28–50 points: Not worth wasting electricity on!
- 51–75 points: Taking out the trash is more fun.
- 76–95 points: Mediocre but not poisonous.
- 96–115 points: Not bad if there's nothing better to do.
- 116–140 points: Sounds like a winner — write the sponsor and say so!

# Index

Page numbers in *italics* indicate illustrations.

104

## About the Authors

MALKA DRUCKER, award-winning author of several children's books, has long been familiar with the television industry. Her parents write and produce TV shows. She lives in Los Angeles with her husband and their two sons.

ELIZABETH JAMES is the author of many books for young people. In addition, she has written for film and television. She and her husband, film producer J. David Marks, live in Beverly Hills, California.